Theory
Made FUN

CD with
Sing-Along Songs

Sing-Along Activity Book

Production: Frank J. Hackinson
Production Coordinators: Peggy Gallagher and Philip Groeber
Editors: Edwin McLean and Peggy Gallagher
Cover and Interior Illustrations: Julia Olson
Engraving: Tempo Music Press, Inc.
Printer: Tempo Music Press, Inc.

ISBN-13: 978-1-56939-939-2

Notes to the Teacher and Parent...

Piano Made FUN for the Young is an early childhood piano curriculum designed to teach and reinforce the basics of piano study, in a spirit of FUN, PLAYFULNESS, and SUCCESS. The curriculum consists of *Sing-Along Activity Books* with CD's and leveled piano books with CD's. It is especially effective in a group setting, but great for private students as well.

Young children enjoy lessons that offer a variety of experiences. This curriculum provides diverse learning opportunities that incorporate singing, movement, games, and more. A typical lesson is divided into two areas:

Rug Time — *Theory Made FUN; Counting Made FUN; Notes Made FUN*

The first portion of each lesson is Rug Time. **The beginning of each unit in the piano books indicates which concepts to cover at Rug Time**. During Rug Time, students sit on the floor near the piano and sing songs using the *Sing-Along Activity Books* to learn and review concepts. Singing the simple songs keeps their attention and helps them have fun while learning. Teachers who are not comfortable singing can use the CD's to listen to the songs with their students. Because the songs are short and easy to remember, many of them can be reviewed in a matter of minutes.

The *Sing-Along Activity Books* with CD's are divided into the categories of THEORY, COUNTING, and NOTES, which keep students focused on the different processes of learning, before putting it all together at the piano. Young children learn best through consistent reinforcement. Concepts are meant to be reviewed over and over each week, giving students a solid foundation.

Throughout the books, the shaded boxes are "teacher explanations" and the italicized words are "student directions." Students can put a check in the Practice Box each time they sing a song and can also color the pictures for an added activity throughout the book. Teachers can use the resources on **www.PianoMadeFun.com** for fun ideas and printable activities that provide extensions that can be used during Rug Time.

Piano Time — *Pre-Reading Made FUN, Starter Book; Note Reading Made FUN, Book 1*

The second portion of each lesson is Piano Time. During Piano Time students use the leveled piano books with CD's to learn to play and read music at a pace that is steady and comfortable. The music is simple and easy to read so young students do not become frustrated. The themed units and play-along CD's make the learning process fun and interesting.

We are confident this curriculum will give young students an effective way to get started with the piano, in an atmosphere they can enjoy!

Remember, you can visit **www.PianoMadeFun.com** for free printables and teaching aids.

Kevin and Julia Olson

FJH2159

Table of Contents

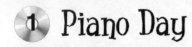

Piano Day

Congratulations on your decision to learn to play the piano! You should try to make every day a *Piano Day*. If you spend a few minutes practicing each day, you will find that playing the piano is really lots of fun.

You can sing this song at the beginning of each lesson.

It's been a great week, yeah, I knew that it would,— and I prac-ticed ev-'ry day, ev-'ry

day that I could.— Though at times it seemed hard,— like I could-n't get it done, but as

soon as I did it I had lots of fun. It's pi-an-o day,— let us shout hur-ray.— We're

Fill out the practice agreement on page 6.

FJH2159

Practice Agreement

My name is [   ]

I will do my best to practice [   ] days a week, [   ] minutes a day.

Signed:

_____   _____
                Student   Parent

PRACTICE BOX *Put a check or a sticker in this box each time you sing the "Piano Day" song.*

FJH2159

Piano Day

2 Beat

Music makes you want to tap your feet because it has a beat, like a beating drum. Listen to the beat in all the music you hear. See if you can clap or tap to the beat.

Clap to the beat as you sing this song. You can also play the beat on a drum or a kitchen pot.

In mu - sic you will hear a beat; to find it you can tap your feet. It's

stead - y like a beat - ing drum, and you will find it's lots of fun.

Tap the drums below with a steady beat.

PRACTICE BOX *Put a check or a sticker in this box each time you sing this song.*

FJH2159

Beat

③ Tempo

The beat in music can be fast, slow, or in the middle. This is called tempo. A metronome can help you set a tempo for your music. You might want to purchase a metronome for practice at home.

Move your arm back and forth to pretend you are a ticking metronome as you sing this song.

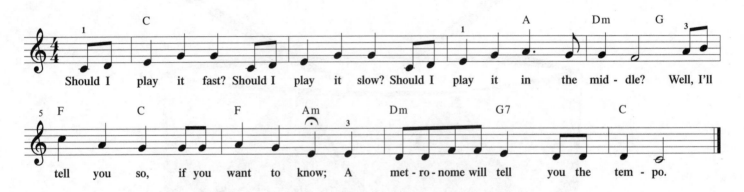

Should I play it fast? Should I play it slow? Should I play it in the mid - dle? Well, I'll tell you so, if you want to know; A met - ro - nome will tell you the tem - po.

Set a metronome to a very high number. Then tap the metronomes below to the beat.

PRACTICE BOX *Put a check or a sticker in this box each time you sing this song.*

FJH2159

Tempo

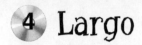

There are many different words to describe the tempo of a piece. The word *largo* means slow, like a tired turtle. Largo is between 40 and 60 on your metronome.

Tap your hands on your legs to the beat and pretend you are a tired turtle as you sing this song.

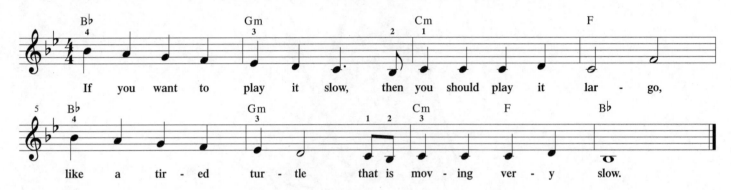

If you want to play it slow, then you should play it lar - go,

like a tir - ed tur - tle that is mov - ing ver - y slow.

Set a metronome to 40 and tap the turtles to the beat. Do they seem slow?

PRACTICE BOX *Put a check or a sticker in this box each time you sing this song.*

FJH2159

Largo

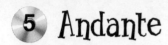

5 Andante

The word *andante* means neither fast nor slow, like sneakers that are walking. Andante is between 76 and 108 on your metronome.

Tap your hands on your legs to the beat and pretend they are walking sneakers as you sing this song.

An - dan - te means to walk, it's nei - ther fast nor slow. Just

play it with a walk - ing speed like sneak - ers on the go.

Set a metronome to 76 and tap the sneakers to the beat. Do they seem fast or slow or neither?

PRACTICE BOX *Put a check or a sticker in this box each time you sing this song.*

14

Andante

6 Allegro

The word *allegro* means fast, like a hungry cheetah. Allegro is between 120 and 168 on your metronome.

Tap your hands on your legs to the beat and pretend you are a hungry cheetah as you sing this song.

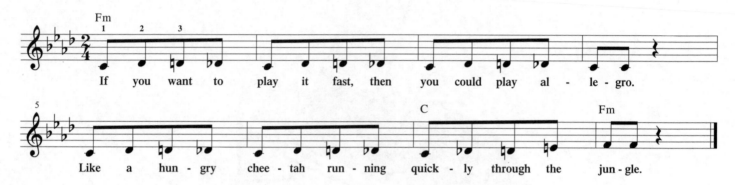

If you want to play it fast, then you could play al - le - gro.

Like a hun - gry chee - tah run - ning quick - ly through the jun - gle.

Set a metronome to 120 and tap the cheetahs to the beat. Do they seem fast?

PRACTICE BOX *Put a check or a sticker in this box each time you sing this song.*

FJH2159

Allegro

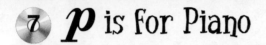 **7** *p* is for Piano

Music can be soft, loud, or in the middle. There are words to describe how soft or loud you should play. These words are called dynamics. *p* is for piano, which means soft.

Wiggle your fingers, moving your hands from left to right and pretend you are a quiet mouse as you sing this song.

*Trace each *p* below.*

 p   *p*   *p*   *p*   *p*

PRACTICE BOX *Put a check or a sticker in this box each time you sing this song.*

FJH215

p is for Piano

 **𝑓 is for Forte**

𝑓 is for forte, which means loud.

Tap your hands loudly on your legs to make the sound of thunder as you sing this song.

𝑓 is for for - te. You should play it nice and loud, just like the thun-der as it rum - bles through a cloud.

Trace each 𝑓 below.

   𝑓   𝑓   𝑓   𝑓

PRACTICE BOX *Put a check or a sticker in this box each time you sing this song.*

𝒎 *is for mezzo—mezzo means medium.*
𝒎𝒇 *is medium loud and* 𝒎𝒑 *is medium soft.*

f is for Forte

⑨ Finger Numbers

Each of our fingers has a number given to it for playing the piano. Thumb is finger number 1. Pointer finger is finger number 2. Tall finger is finger number 3. Ring finger is finger number 4. Pinky is finger number 5.

Raise your hands high in the air, moving them from left to right and wiggle the correct fingers when you sing the finger numbers.

Wiggle the finger numbers that are indicated below. Trace the finger numbers on the next page.

1 5 3 2 4 5 2 3 1 4

PRACTICE BOX *Put a check or a sticker in this box each time you sing this song.*

Finger Numbers

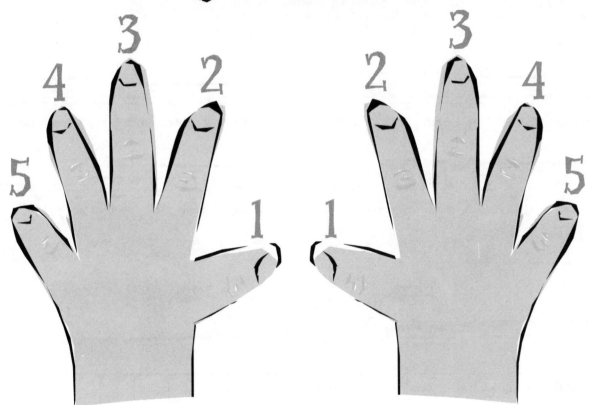

10 Spider Fingers

When you place your fingers on the piano keyboard, pretend your hands are like spiders sitting on big bubbles. Curve your "spider fingers" over the bubble and try not to pop it when you play.

Pretend your hands are like spiders moving across the piano keys as you sing this song.

When you play, re - mem - ber that you should not play with fin - gers flat.

Think of spi - ders on the keys, curv - ing 'round a bub - ble, please.

Draw a bubble under each spider below.

PRACTICE BOX *Put a check or a sticker in this box each time you sing this song.*

FJH2159

Spider Fingers

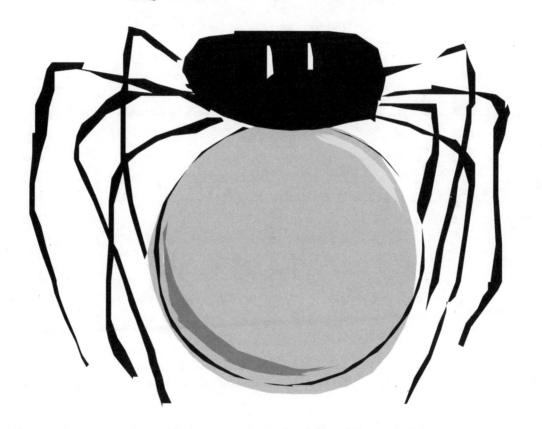

⑪ The Black Keys

Did you ever notice that the piano keyboard looks like a zebra? There are white keys and black keys that look like stripes. The black keys are in groups of 2 and 3. The high notes are to the right and the low notes are to the left.

Clap to the beat as you sing the beginning of this song. When you come to "one, two, one, two, three," try playing the black keys with your finger number 2 or tap your finger on the keyboard on the next page.

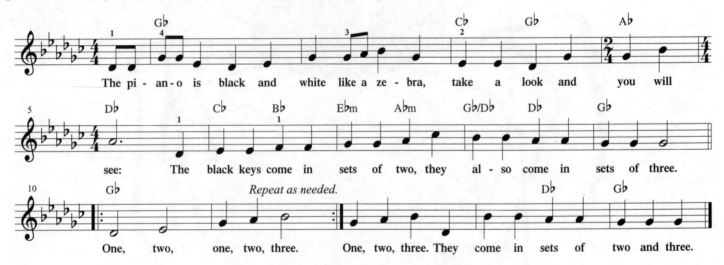

The pi - an - o is black and white like a ze - bra, take a look and you will

see: The black keys come in sets of two, they al - so come in sets of three.

One, two, one, two, three. *Repeat as needed.* One, two, three. They come in sets of two and three.

PRACTICE BOX *Put a check or a sticker in this box each time you sing this song.*

FJH2159

The Black Keys

ONE   TWO   ONE   TWO   THREE

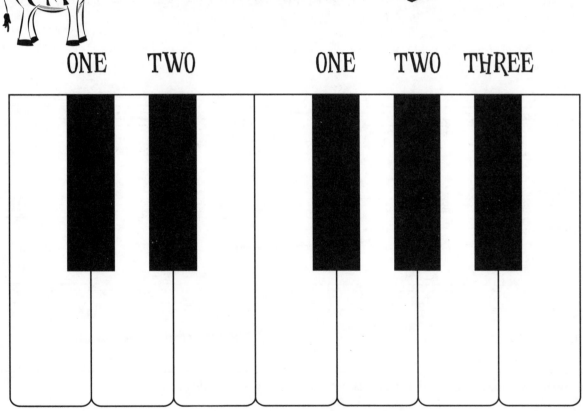

12 The Musical Alphabet

The musical alphabet is different than the regular alphabet. The musical alphabet starts on A but only goes up to G. Then starts all over at A again and is repeated over and over on the white keys. Notice that G and A are neighbors in the musical alphabet.

Clap to the beat as you sing the beginning of this song. When you come to "ABCDEFG," try playing the white keys with your finger number 2 or tap your finger on the keyboard on the next page.

Trace the letters on the white keys on page 29.

PRACTICE BOX *Put a check or a sticker in this box each time you sing this song.*

FJH2159

The Musical Alphabet

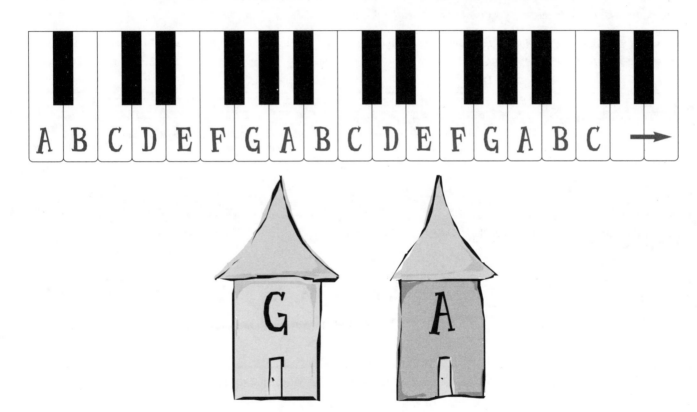

13 The White Keys

You might think it is impossible to learn all those white keys on the piano since there are actually more than fifty of them. It is easy though, if you find the black key groups first. Below each 2-black-key-group you will always find CDE, and below each 3-black-key-group you will always find FGAB.

Clap to the beat as you sing the beginning of this song. When you come to the "2-black-keys, then CDE" and "3-black-keys, then FGAB,"
try playing them on your piano or tap your fingers on the keyboard on the next page.

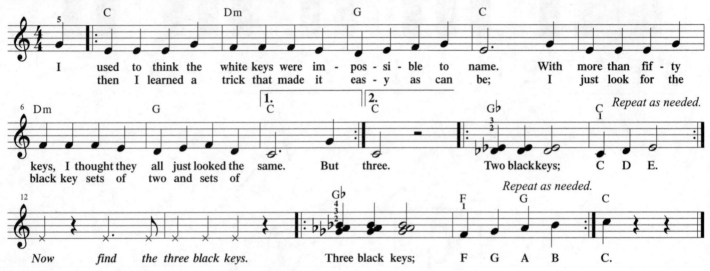

Trace the letters on the white keys on page 31.

PRACTICE BOX *Put a check or a sticker in this box each time you sing this song.*

The White Keys

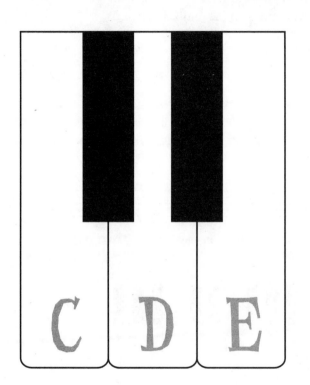

14 Octave

Did you know that an octopus has 8 legs and that an octagon has 8 sides? Well, on the piano keyboard, a note is repeated every 8 keys and this is called an octave. If you start on "A" and count up to 8, then you will land on "A" again. If you start on "B" and count up to 8, then you will land on "B" again. This continues for every note up the entire keyboard.

Wiggle 8 fingers and pretend your hands are an octopus at the beginning of this song. Point to the keys on the keyboard as you sing "8 notes in an octave."

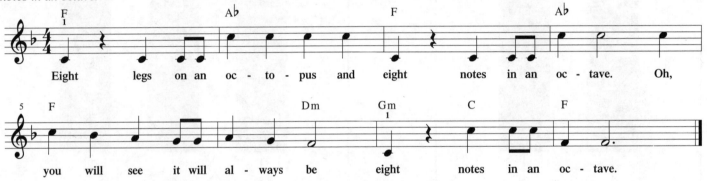

Circle each "C" on the keyboard below. Trace the "C's" and numbers on page 33.

PRACTICE BOX *Put a check or a sticker in this box each time you sing this song.*

FJH2159

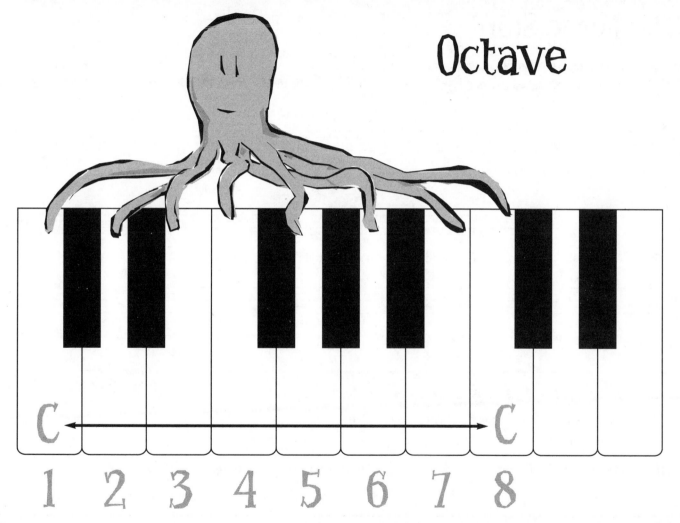

Octave

Music notes are written on a group of lines and spaces called a staff. A staff has 5 lines and 4 spaces. Piano music is written on two staves (staffs) grouped together called the grand staff. The top staff is called the treble staff and the bottom staff is called the bass staff.

Trace the numbers on the staff on page 35.

PRACTICE BOX *Put a check or a sticker in this box each time you sing this song.*

34

FJH2159

The Music Staff

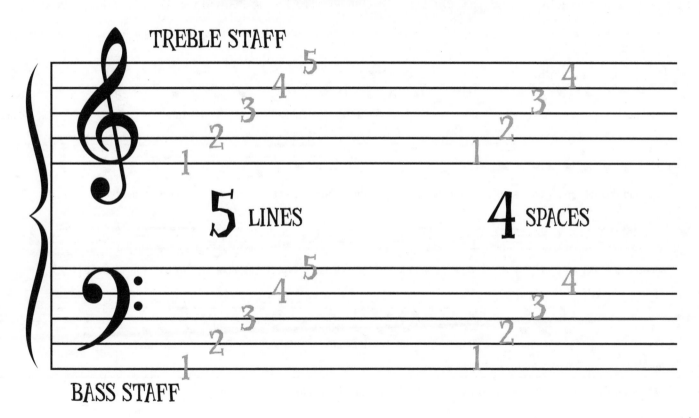

TREBLE STAFF

5 LINES

4 SPACES

BASS STAFF

16 Time Signature

At the beginning of your music, you will see a time signature. The top number tells you how many counts are in each measure and the bottom number tells you the type of note that gets the count. (For now it will usually be the quarter note.)

Clap to the beat as you sing this song. On the next page, tap the top number when you sing about it and tap the bottom number when you sing about it.

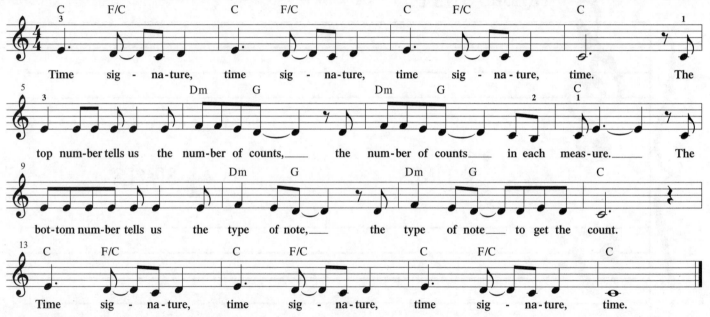

Trace the numbers on the time signature on page 37.

PRACTICE BOX *Put a check or a sticker in this box each time you sing this song.*

 FJH2159

Time Signature

$$\frac{2}{4} \qquad \frac{3}{4} \qquad \frac{4}{4}$$

🔘 17 Right Hand / Left Hand

The right hand usually plays the notes written on the treble staff and the left hand usually plays the notes written on the bass staff.

Hold up your right hand when you sing "right hand" and hold up your left hand when you sing "left hand."

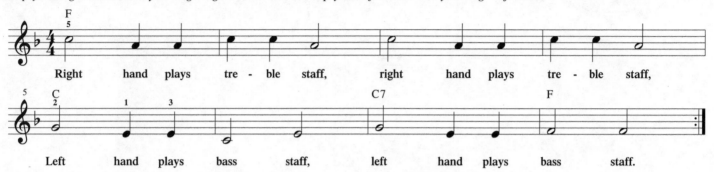

Right hand plays tre - ble staff, right hand plays tre - ble staff,

Left hand plays bass staff, left hand plays bass staff.

Trace the clefs on this page and page 39.

PRACTICE BOX *Put a check or a sticker in this box each time you sing this song.*

38

Bass

Treble

18 Step

Music notes can move in steps, which is line to space or space to line on the music staff.

Point to the stepping notes on the next page as you sing this song.

Line   to   space   or   space   to   line,   a   step   is   eas - y   ev - 'ry   time.

Circle the steps below.

PRACTICE BOX *Put a check or a sticker in this box each time you sing this song.*

FJH2159

Step

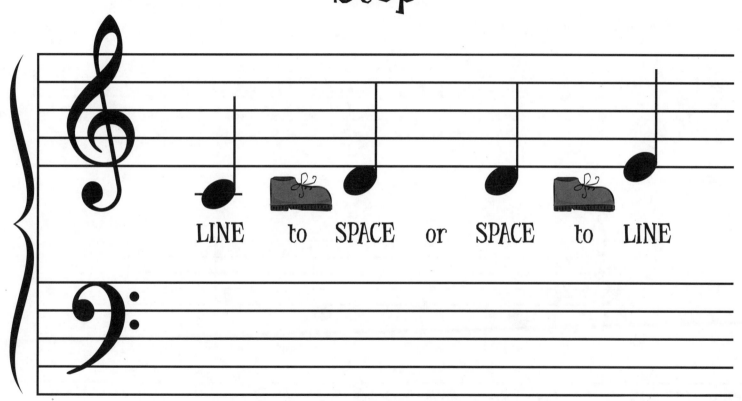

LINE   to   SPACE   or   SPACE   to   LINE

19 Skip

Music notes can move in skips, which is line to line or space to space on the music staff.

Point to the skipping notes on the next page as you sing this song.

Line to line or space to space, a skip will help you win the race.

Circle the skips below.

PRACTICE BOX *Put a check or a sticker in this box each time you sing this song.*

FJH2159

Skip

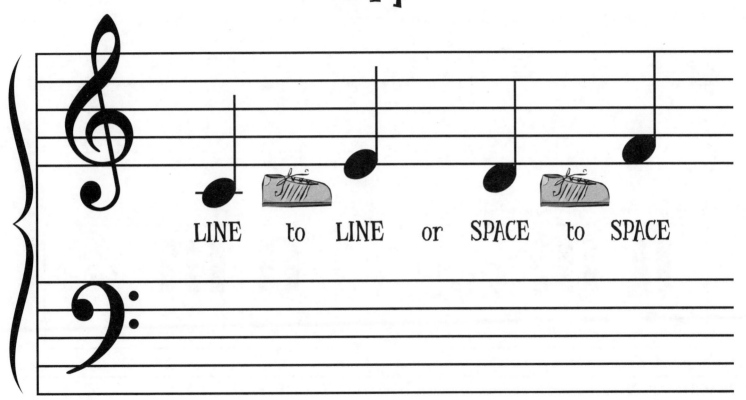

LINE to LINE or SPACE to SPACE

20 Interval

You can measure the distance between two notes on a staff or the keyboard. This is called an interval.

Place your finger on the ruler and slide it up as you sing "interval." Tap the keys as you sing "the distance between two notes."

In - ter - val, in - ter - val: The dis-tance be-tween two

notes, two notes; The dis-tance be-tween two notes.

Color the dots and trace the interval names below.

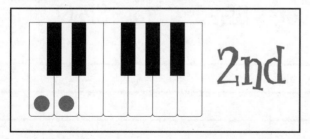

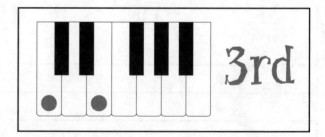

Color the picture on page 45.

PRACTICE BOX *Put a check or a sticker in this box each time you sing this song.*

FJH2159

Interval

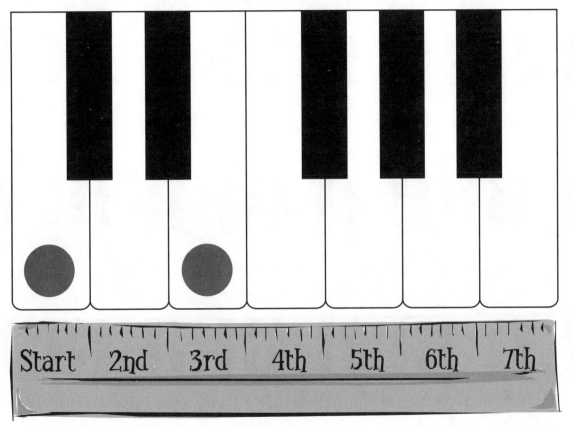

On these pages, you can find and color the different keys that you have learned in this book.
Try making a piano rainbow. Color each C red, D orange, E yellow, F green, G blue, A purple, and B pink.
You can also print more of these pages at www.PianoMadeFun.com.

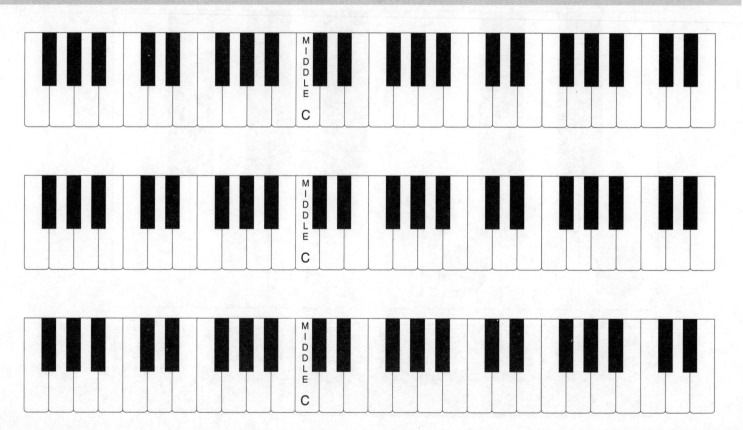

FJH2159

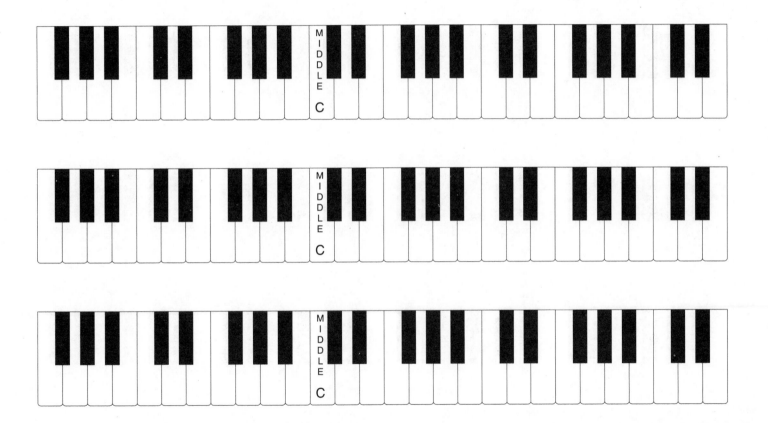

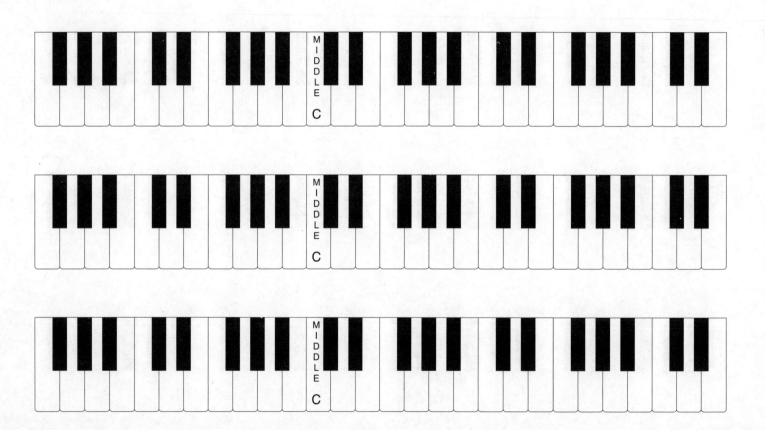

FJH2159